MY FIRST
COOK
B·O·O·K

Angela Wilkes

Dorling Kindersley • London

Design Roger Priddy

Photography David Johnson
Home Economist Dolly Meers
Editor Jane Elliot

First published in Great Britain in 1989
by Dorling Kindersley Limited,
9 Henrietta Street, London SW2E 8PS
Reprinted 1989
Reprinted with revisions 1990, 1993
Reprinted 1990 (twice), 1992, 1993, 1994

British Library Cataloguing in Publication Data

Wilkes, Angela
    My first cook book.
    1. Food – Recipes
    I. Title
    641.5

    ISBN 0-86318-356-5

Phototypeset by Tradespools Ltd, Frome, Somerset
Reproduced in Singapore by Bright Arts
Printed in Italy by L.E.G.O.

Dorling Kindersley would like to thank Henrietta Winthrop,
Pamela Cowan, Dan Bristow, Isobel Bulat and
Nancy Graham for their help in producing this book.

CONTENTS

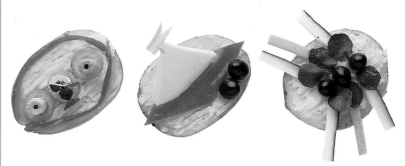

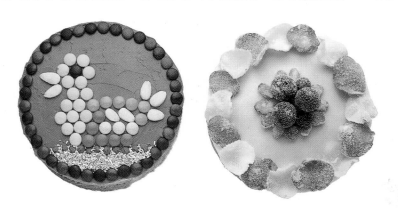

COOKING BY PICTURES

My First Cook Book shows you step-by-step how to make all sorts of delicious things to eat. Easy-to-follow recipes show you which ingredients you need, what to do with them and what the finished food should look like – life size! Every recipe is followed by lots of colourful ideas on how to decorate what you have made. Below are the points to look for in each recipe and opposite is an important list of cook's rules to read before you start.

How to use this book

The ingredients
All the ingredients you need for each recipe are shown life-size, to help you check you have the right amounts.

Increasing the quantity
Each recipe tells you how many things the ingredients make. To make more, double or treble the quantities.

Cook's tools
These illustrated checklists show you which utensils you need to have ready before you start cooking.

SPICY BISCUITS

You can make spicy biscuits in all kinds of different shapes. You can make them for parties or just for tea. The ingredients shown here will make about twenty-five biscuits. On the next four pages you can find out how to cut out and decorate your biscuits.

You will need

75 g (3 oz) butter

1 small egg

275 g (10 oz) plain flour

50 g (2 oz) golden syrup

1 level teaspoon baking powder

100 g (4oz) soft brown sugar

1 dessertspoon cinnamon

COOK'S TOOLS

Wooden spoon

Mixing bowl   Rolling pin

Measuring jug   Sieve   Biscuit cutters

Knife

Fork

Palette knife   Baking tray

Making the biscuit dough

1 Set oven at 170°C/ 325°F/ Gas Mark 3. Sift the flour and cinnamon into the mixing bowl, then stir in the sugar.

2 Add the butter and cut it up. Rub the flour and butter together with your fingertips until the mixture looks like breadcrumbs.

3 Break the egg into a jug and beat it with a fork. Add the golden syrup and mix it with the egg until smooth.

4 Make a hollow in the flour and pour in the egg mixture. Mix everything together well until you have a big ball of dough.

5 Put the ball of dough into a plastic bag. Place it in the fridge for 30 minutes, which will make it easier to roll out.

6 Sprinkle some flour on a table and your rolling pin. Roll out the dough evenly until it is about 0.5 cm (¼ in) thick.

Turn the page to see what to do next.

Cook's rules

1 Do not cook anything unless there is an adult there to help you.

2 Read each recipe before you start, to make sure you have everything you need.

3 Wash your hands and put on an apron before you start cooking.

4 Carefully weigh or measure all the ingredients you use.

5 Always wear oven gloves when picking up anything hot, or when putting things into or taking them out of the oven.

6 Be very careful with sharp knives.

7 Turn saucepan handles to the side of the cooker, so that you do not knock them.

8 Never leave the kitchen while electric or gas rings are turned on.

9 Always turn the oven off when you have finished cooking.

Step-by-step
Step-by-step photographs and clear instructions show you what to do at every stage of the recipe.

The oven glove symbol
Whenever you see this symbol by a picture or instruction, it means you should ask an adult for help.

The finishing touches
Life-size pictures show you how to decorate the things you have made and which ingredients to use.

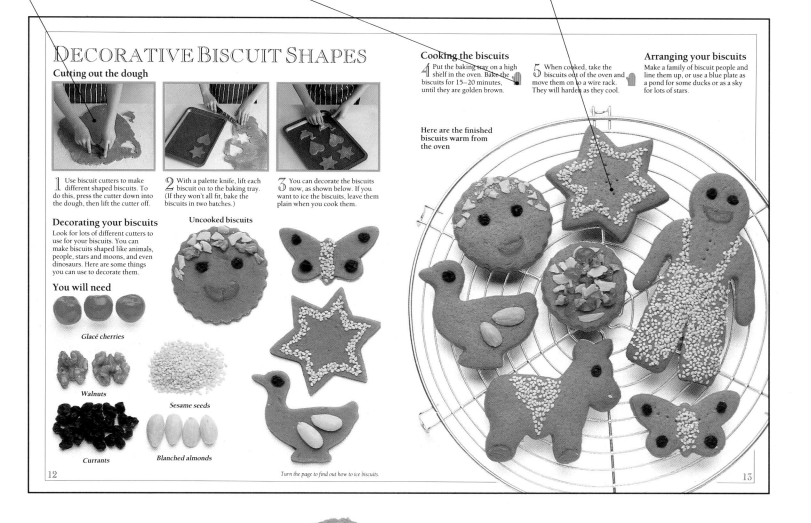

DECORATIVE BISCUIT SHAPES

Cutting out the dough

1 Use biscuit cutters to make different shaped biscuits. To do this, press the cutter down into the dough, then lift the cutter off.

2 With a palette knife, lift each biscuit on to the baking tray. (If they won't all fit, bake the biscuits in two batches.)

3 You can decorate the biscuits now, as shown below. If you want to ice the biscuits, leave them plain when you cook them.

Decorating your biscuits

Look for lots of different cutters to use for your biscuits. You can make biscuits shaped like animals, people, stars and moons, and even dinosaurs. Here are some things you can use to decorate them.

You will need

Glacé cherries

Walnuts

Sesame seeds

Currants

Blanched almonds

Uncooked biscuits

Cooking the biscuits

4 Put the baking tray on a high shelf in the oven. Bake the biscuits for 15–20 minutes, until they are golden brown.

5 When cooked, take the biscuits out of the oven and move them on to a wire rack. They will harden as they cool.

Arranging your biscuits

Make a family of biscuit people and line them up, or use a blue plate as a pond for some ducks or as a sky for lots of stars.

Here are the finished biscuits warm from the oven

Turn the page to find out how to ice biscuits.

12

13

COOK'S TOOLS

Here and on the next three pages are all the utensils you will need to follow the recipes in this book. You will also need some kitchen scales, so that you can weigh the ingredients. To make it easy for you to check that you have everything you need before you start cooking, you will find a checklist of cook's tools at the beginning of every recipe.

Pastry brush

Small bowl

Sieve

Mixing bowl

Wooden spoon

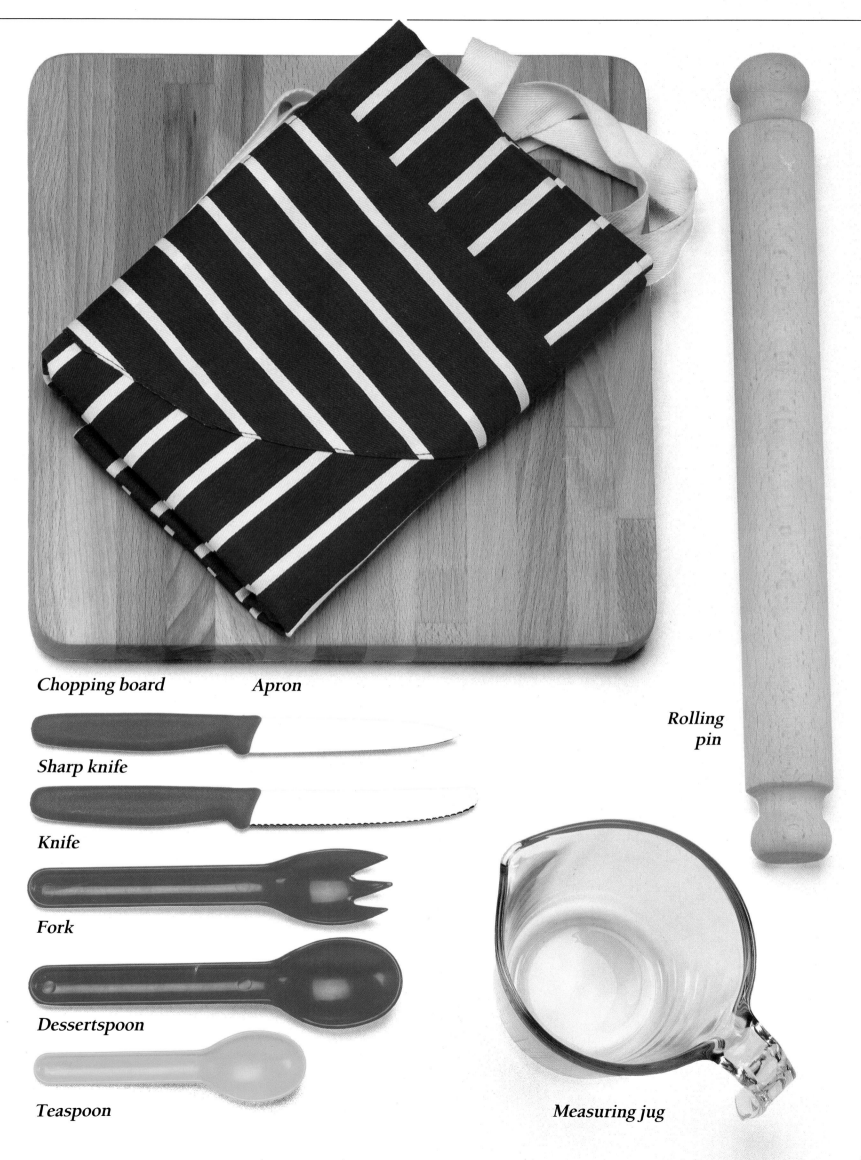

Chopping board   Apron

Sharp knife

Knife

Fork

Dessertspoon

Teaspoon

Rolling
pin

Measuring jug

7

MORE COOK'S TOOLS

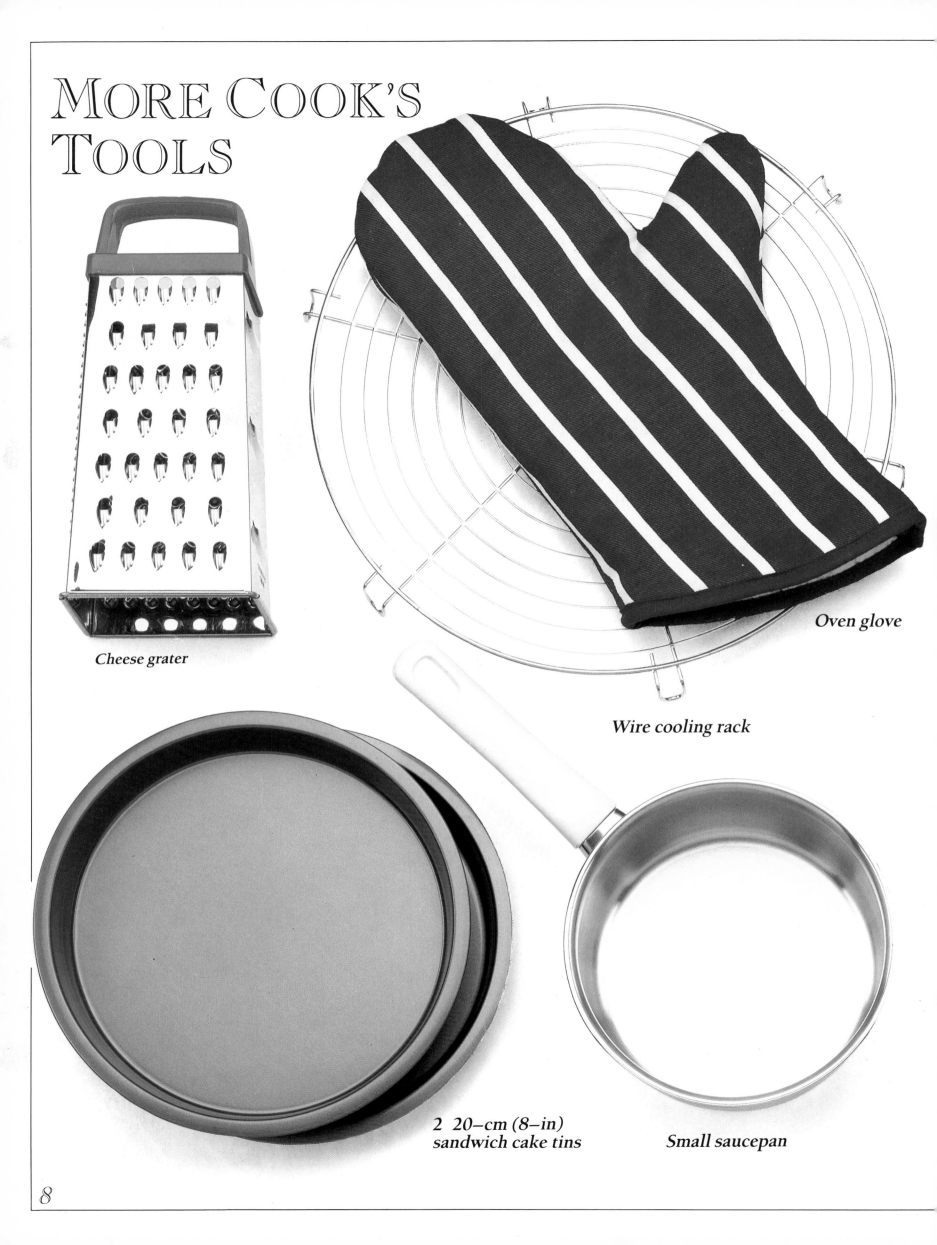

Cheese grater

Oven glove

Wire cooling rack

2 20–cm (8–in) sandwich cake tins

Small saucepan

8

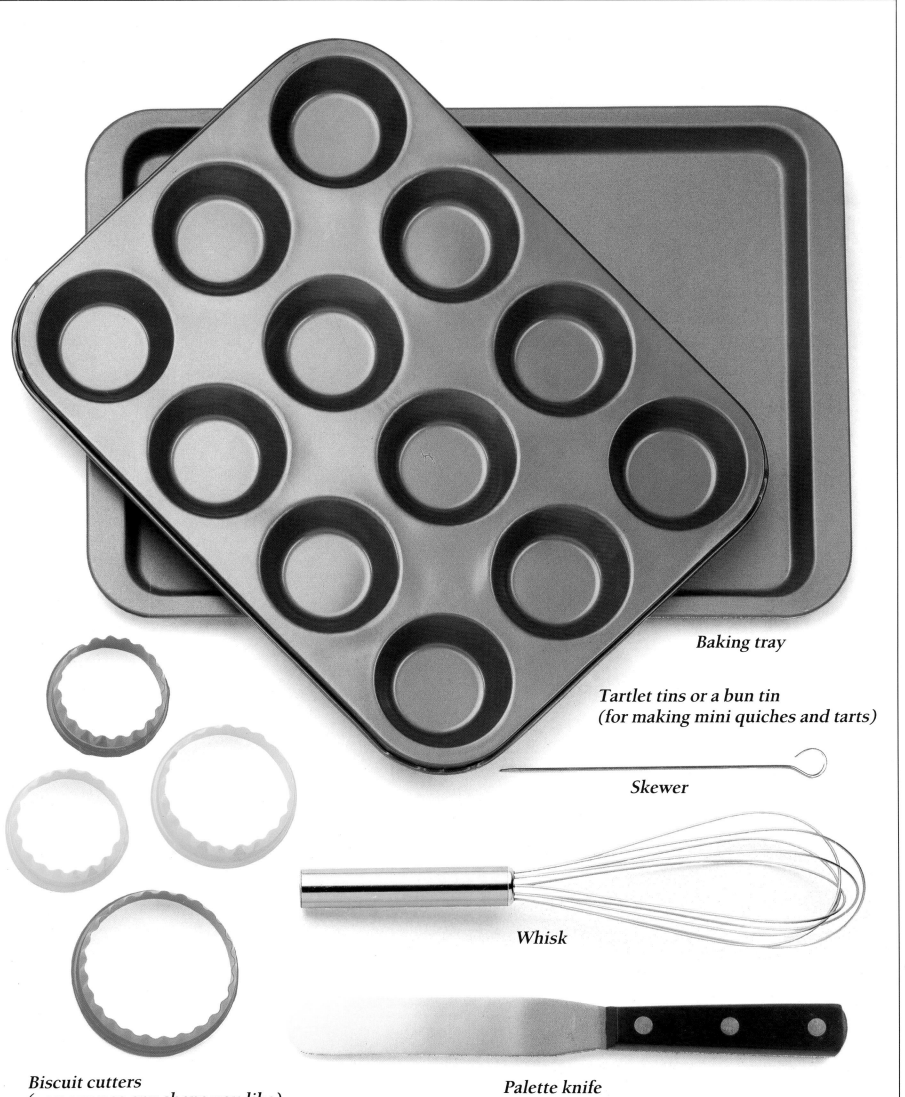

Baking tray

Tartlet tins or a bun tin
(for making mini quiches and tarts)

Skewer

Whisk

Biscuit cutters
(you can use any shape you like)

Palette knife

9

SPICY BISCUITS

You can make spicy biscuits in all kinds of different shapes. You can make them for parties or just for tea. The ingredients shown here will make about twenty-five biscuits. On the next four pages you can find out how to cut out and decorate your biscuits.

You will need

75 g (3 oz) butter

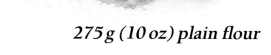

1 small egg

275 g (10 oz) plain flour

Making the biscuit dough

1 Set the oven at 170°C/325°F/ Gas Mark 3. Sift the flour, baking powder and cinammon into a mixing bowl. Stir in the sugar.

2 Add the butter and cut it up. Rub the flour and butter together with your fingertips until the mixture looks like breadcrumbs.

3 Break the egg into a jug and beat it with a fork. Add the golden syrup and mix it with the egg until smooth.

50 g (2 oz) golden syrup

1 level teaspoon
baking powder

1 dessertspoon cinnamon

100 g (4oz) soft brown sugar

4 Make a hollow in the flour and pour in the egg mixture. Mix everything together well until you have a big ball of dough.

5 Put the ball of dough into a plastic bag. Place it in the fridge for 30 minutes, which will make it easier to roll out.

6 Sprinkle some flour on a table and your rolling pin. Roll out the dough evenly until it is about 0.5 cm (¼ in) thick.

Turn the page to see what to do next.

DECORATIVE BISCUIT SHAPES

Cutting out the dough

1 Use biscuit cutters to make different shaped biscuits. To do this, press the cutter down into the dough, then lift the cutter off.

2 With a palette knife, lift each biscuit on to the baking tray. (If they won't all fit, bake the biscuits in two batches.)

3 You can decorate the biscuits now, as shown below. If you want to ice the biscuits, leave them plain when you cook them.

Decorating your biscuits

Look for lots of different cutters to use for your biscuits. You can make biscuits shaped like animals, people, stars and moons, and even dinosaurs. Here are some things you can use to decorate them.

Uncooked biscuits

You will need

Glacé cherries

Walnuts

Sesame seeds

Currants

Blanched almonds

Turn the page to find out how to ice biscuits.

Cooking the biscuits

4 Put the baking tray on a high shelf in the oven. Bake the biscuits for 15–20 minutes, until they are golden brown.

5 When cooked, take the biscuits out of the oven and move them on to a wire rack. They will harden as they cool.

Arranging your biscuits

Make a family of biscuit people and line them up, or use a blue plate as a pond for some ducks or as a sky for lots of stars.

Here are the finished biscuits warm from the oven

13

EASY ICING

To make fancier biscuits you can ice them before decorating them. You must cook the biscuits plain and make sure that they have cooled completely before icing them. Below you can find out how to make white icing and chocolate flavoured icing.

Sieve

Small bowl

Knife

Wooden spoon

25 g (1 oz) cocoa powder (for chocolate icing only)

You will need

1 tablespoon hot water

Glacé cherries

100 g (4 oz) icing sugar

Making the icing

1 Sift the icing sugar into the small bowl. Add the water a little at a time, mixing it with the sugar to make a smooth paste.

2 To make chocolate icing, use 75 g (3 oz) icing sugar and cocoa powder and make it the same way as the white icing.

3 Spoon a little icing on to each biscuit and spread it out evenly with a wet knife. Don't worry if it dribbles down the edges a bit.

Decorating the biscuits

4 Before the icing sets, decorate your biscuits with any of the things shown below. You can make patterns on them, or decorate them to look like faces or animals. Here are some ideas to try.

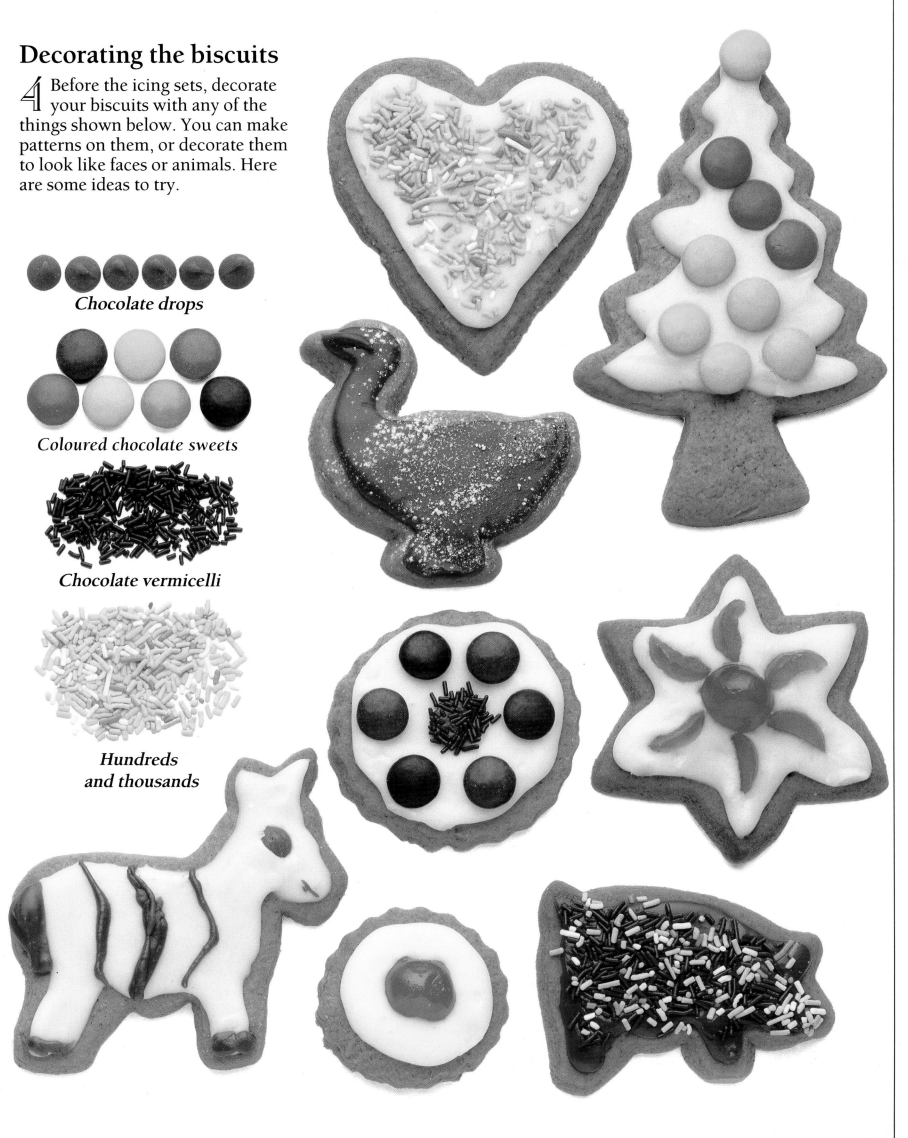

Chocolate drops

Coloured chocolate sweets

Chocolate vermicelli

Hundreds and thousands

ICE CREAM SUNDAES

Ice cream sundaes are great fun to make. All you need is ice cream, some sauces and lots of tasty things to put on top. You must make sundaes quite fast, so that they don't melt. Put them in the fridge as you finish them, or eat them at once! On the next two pages there are some ideas for making silly sundaes.

You will need

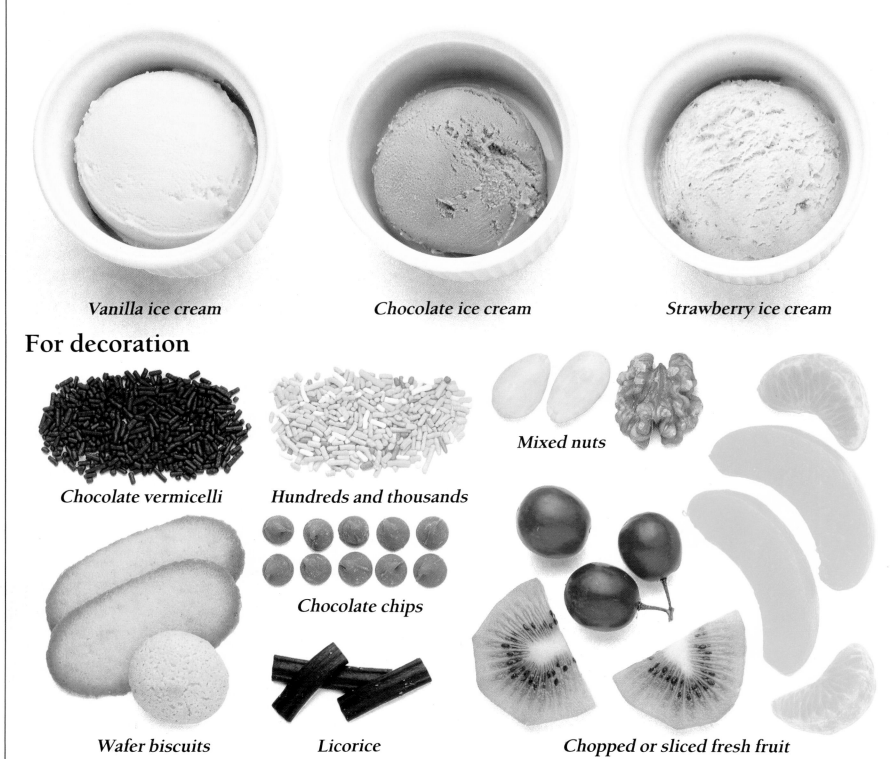

Vanilla ice cream

Chocolate ice cream

Strawberry ice cream

For decoration

Chocolate vermicelli

Hundreds and thousands

Mixed nuts

Chocolate chips

Wafer biscuits

Licorice

Chopped or sliced fresh fruit

16

Making the sauces
For raspberry sauce

150 g (6 oz) raspberries (frozen or fresh)

75 g (3 oz) caster sugar

For chocolate sauce

100 g (4 oz) plain chocolate

Raspberry sauce

1 Wash the raspberries and put them in a sieve over a bowl. Then push the raspberries through the sieve using a wooden spoon.

2 Add the caster sugar to the raspberry pulp a little at a time. Then stir the sauce vigorously until all the sugar has dissolved.

Chocolate sauce

1 Break up the chocolate. Put it in the small bowl with the water. Heat some water in the saucepan until it gently bubbles.

2 Place the bowl over the saucepan until the chocolate melts. Turn off the heat and stir the chocolate until smooth.

3 tablespoons water

Now turn the page for decorating ideas.

SILLY SUNDAES

You can make sundaes that look like colourful insects and a flower, by using the ingredients and sauces shown on the last two pages, or you can experiment with ideas of your own. First put the ice cream in the dishes, then add the sauces and finally the topping ingredients. You will find it easier to scoop ice cream out of containers if you use a metal spoon that you dip into a jug of hot water between each scoop.

BUMBLE-BEE ICE

Chocolate sauce

Chocolate-drop eyes

Vanilla ice cream

Wafer-biscuit wings

Sliced peaches

BUTTERFLY ICE CREAM

Chocolate-drop eyes

Almonds

Licorice antennae

Hundreds and thousands

Sliced pineapple wings

Chocolate drops

FRUITY FLOWER
(for two people)

Chocolate ice cream

Grapes

Sliced peach

Sliced strawberry

18

CATERPILLAR ICE
(for three people)

Use one ball each of chocolate, strawberry and vanilla ice cream.

Raspberry sauce

Licorice antennae

Cherry nose

Wafer biscuit

Chocolate drop

Eyes made of halved grapes

LADYBIRD ICE CREAM

Raspberry sauce

Chopped nuts

Sliced kiwi fruit

Strawberry ice cream

Grape eyes

Licorice

Raspberry sauce

Strawberry ice cream

Chocolate-drop spots

19

Cheesy Potato Boats

Stuffed potatoes are a meal in themselves and are easy to make. Here are some unusual ideas on how to decorate them once you have cooked them. Potatoes take a long time to cook, so put them in the oven 1 to 1½ hours before you want to eat them*.

For two people you will need

2 knobs of butter

50 g (2 oz) grated cheese

1 large scrubbed potato

For decoration you can use any of these things

Button mushrooms

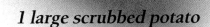

Strips of cucumber

Stoned black olives

Carrots, sliced or cut into sticks

Sliced cheese cut into shapes

COOK'S TOOLS

Small bowl

Knife

Fork

Tablespoon

Cheese grater

Greased baking tray

Sliced peppers, cut into strips

Shredded lettuce

Watercress

20

* Ask an adult to check if the potatoes are cooked. Leave the oven on for step 3.

Cooking the potatoes

1 Set the oven at 200°C/400°F/ Gas Mark 6. Prick the potatoes and place them on the greased baking tray. Bake for 1¼ hours*.

2 When cooked, cut the potatoes in half lengthways. Scoop out the middles into the bowl and mash them. Stir in the butter and cheese.

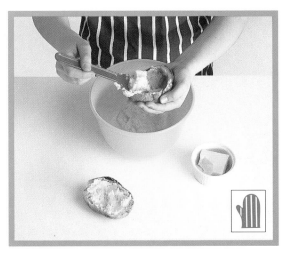

3 Spoon the mixture back into the potato skins and level them off. Then put them back into the oven for another 15 minutes.

*Carefully prick the potatoes using a fork or skewer.

Decorating the potatoes

You can decorate the potatoes once they have been cooked for a second time. Make them into sailing boats, steamer ships or rowing boats as shown here.

SAILING JACKET

Yellow pepper flag

Cocktail-stick mast

Cheese sail

Red pepper deck

POTATO ROWING BOAT

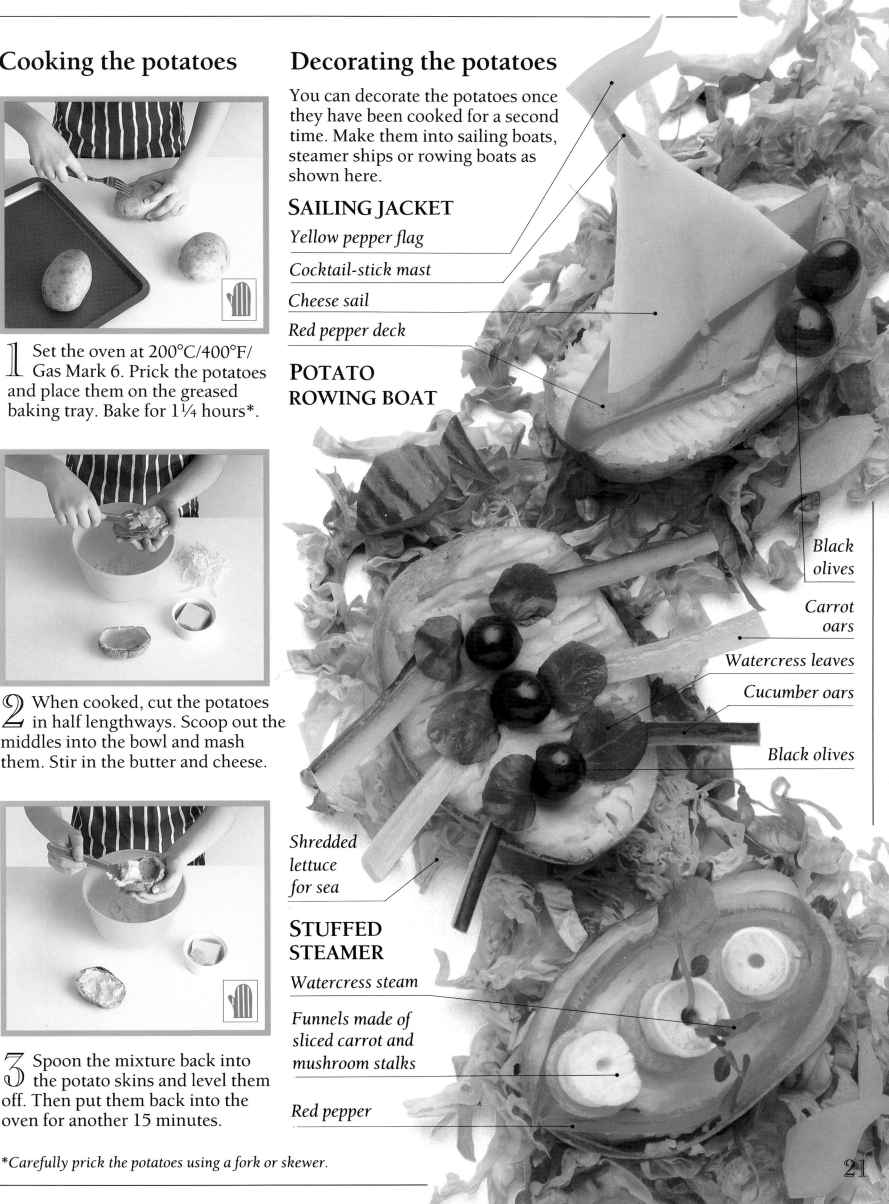

Black olives

Carrot oars

Watercress leaves

Cucumber oars

Black olives

Shredded lettuce for sea

STUFFED STEAMER

Watercress steam

Funnels made of sliced carrot and mushroom stalks

Red pepper

SPEEDY PIZZA

This pizza is quick and easy to make. Here you can see how to make the pizza and sauce, and on the next page are some ideas for toppings. You can make two 10 cm (4 in) pizzas from the ingredients below.

You will need for the pizza

A pinch of salt

150 g (6 oz)
self-raising flour

40 g (1½ oz) butter

3–4 tablespoons milk

50 g (2 oz)
grated cheese

COOK'S TOOLS

Mixing bowl

Small
saucepan

Wooden spoon

Rolling pin

Knife

Cheese
grater

Sharp knife*

Chopping board   Baking tray

For the sauce

1 small onion

1 dessertspoon
tomato purée

A pinch each of
salt and pepper

1 small tin tomatoes

Make sure that an adult helps you when you are using a sharp knife.

Making the sauce

1 Set the oven at 220°C/425°F/ Gas Mark 7. Peel the onion, then cut it in half and chop it up finely on the chopping board.

2 Put the chopped onion in the saucepan. Add the tomatoes, tomato purée, the salt and pepper and stir the mixture together.

3 Cook the mixture over a low heat for about 15 minutes, stirring from time to time. Then turn off the heat and let it cool.

Making the dough

1 While the sauce is cooking, make the dough. Put the flour, salt and butter in the mixing bowl. Cut the butter into small pieces.

2 Rub the pieces of butter into the flour between your fingertips and thumbs until the mixture looks like breadcrumbs.

3 Add the grated cheese and milk to the flour mixture. Mix everything together until you have a smooth ball of dough.

4 Divide the dough in two and make each into a ball. Roll each ball of dough into a circular shape about 10 cm (4 in) across.

5 Lay the circles of dough on the greased baking tray. Spoon the tomato sauce on to them, spreading it out evenly to the edges.

6 Decorate the pizzas (see next page). Put them in the oven to cook for 15–20 minutes, until the edges are golden brown.

Now turn the page.

PARTY PIZZAS

Once you have made the basic pizzas, you can turn them into picture pizzas, using any of the ingredients below, before cooking them. Try making one of the pizzas shown here, or experiment with ideas of your own.

Topping ingredients

Grated cheese

Sliced ham cut into strips

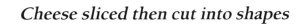
Sliced peppers

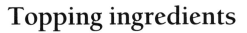

Stoned black olives

Cheese sliced then cut into shapes

Sliced cooked sausage

ITALIAN PIZZA

Sliced mushrooms

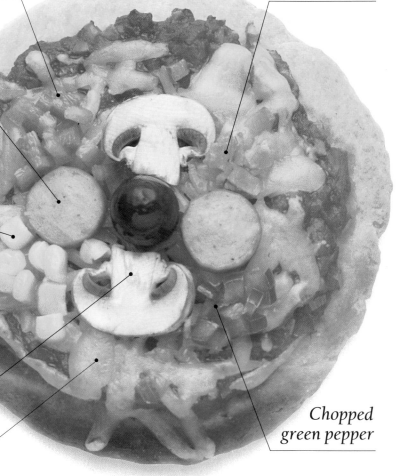

Chopped red pepper

Sliced cooked sausage

Chopped ham

Sweetcorn

Sliced mushroom

Grated cheese

Chopped green pepper

Tinned sweetcorn

24

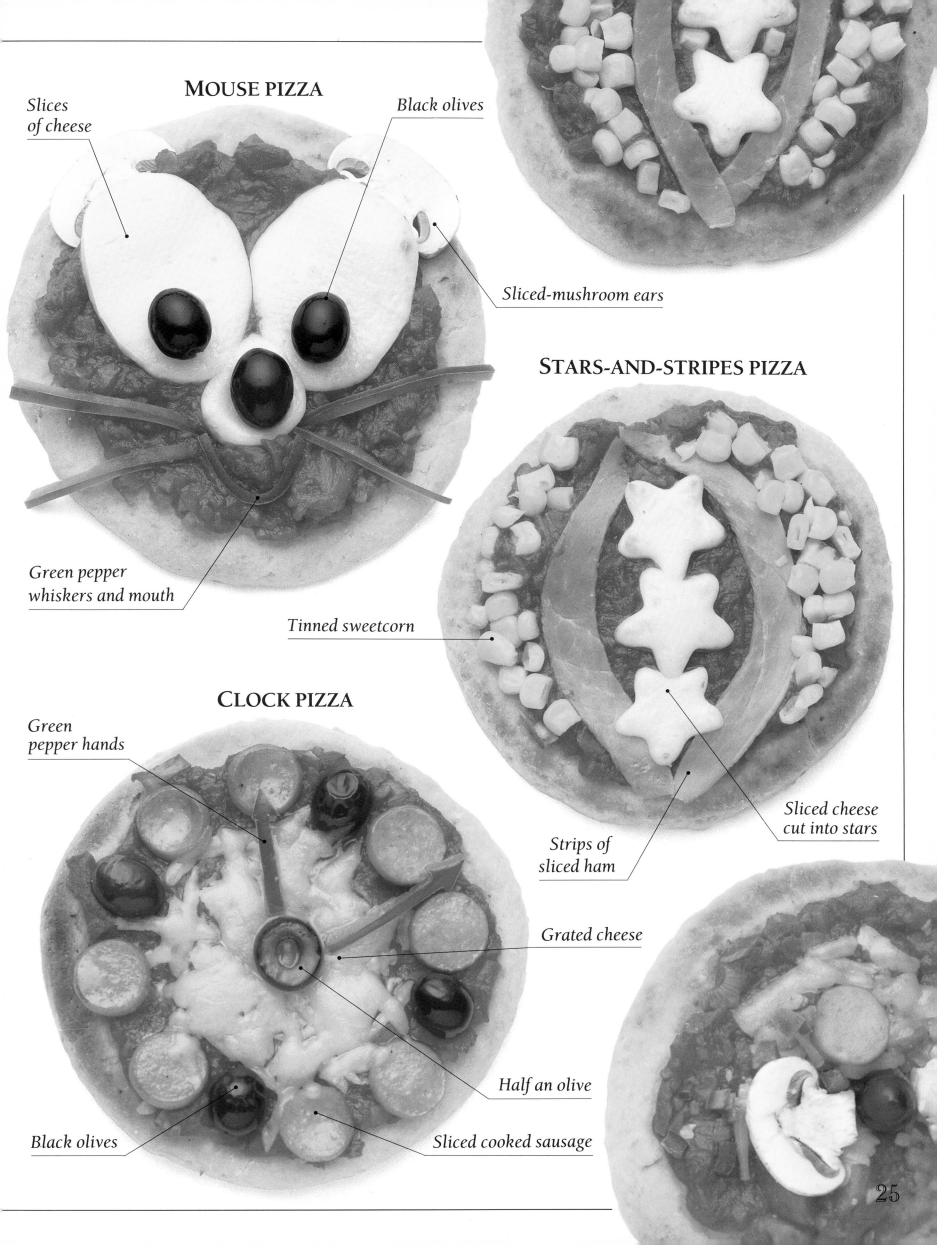

MOUSE PIZZA

Slices of cheese

Black olives

Sliced-mushroom ears

Green pepper whiskers and mouth

STARS-AND-STRIPES PIZZA

Tinned sweetcorn

Sliced cheese cut into stars

Strips of sliced ham

CLOCK PIZZA

Green pepper hands

Grated cheese

Half an olive

Black olives

Sliced cooked sausage

25

FRUIT FOOLS

You can make fruit fools with any fruit soft enough to mash with a fork. Here you can see how to make strawberry or banana fool. The amount of fruit shown for either sort will make four small fools.

You will need

¼ litre (½ pint)
double cream
or yoghurt

A wedge
of lemon*

25 g (1 oz) caster sugar

2 small bananas

OR 220 g (8 oz) strawberries

For decoration

COOK'S TOOLS

Bowl

Serving dishes

Knife

Fork

Whisk   Wooden spoon

Chocolate buttons

Seedless grapes

Wafer biscuits

Glacé cherries

Sliced kiwi fruit

*A few drops of lemon juice will stop the banana fool losing its colour.

What you do

1 Cut the strawberries in half or peel and slice the bananas. Put the fruit in the bowl and mash it with a fork until it is smooth.

2 Whisk the cream or yogurt until it is thick and creamy. Add this and the sugar to the mashed fruit. Stir them in well.

3 Pour the fruit mixture into the serving dishes or glasses. Decorate them as shown below, or however you like.

BEAR FOOL

FOOLISH DOG

The banana-fool bear has biscuit ears, eyes made of biscuits and chocolate drops, a cherry nose and a slice of kiwi fruit for a mouth

The strawberry-fool dog has sliced strawberry ears, eyes made of grapes, a biscuit and chocolate-drop nose, and whiskers made of kiwi fruit.

FLOWERING FOOL

The flower pattern on this strawberry fool is made of sliced kiwi fruit and glacé cherries arranged around a grape in the middle.

Quick Bread

Making bread is great fun. This recipe makes enough dough for eight rolls. Here you can see how to make the dough. The next two pages show you how to make and decorate the rolls. Turn to page 32 and see how to make a whole family of bears.

You will need

3 g (½ sachet) quick-action dried yeast

1 dessertspoon vegetable or sunflower oil

A large pinch of salt

COOK'S TOOLS

Mixing bowl

Measuring jug

Kitchen scissors

Pastry brush

Wooden spoon

Greased baking tray

Wire rack

Making the dough

1 Set the oven to 230°C/450°F/
Gas Mark 8. Put the flour,
yeast and salt in the mixing bowl.
Add the vegetable oil and water.

2 Mix everything together into a
firm dough. If the dough is
sticky, add a little flour. Add a little
water if it is too dry.

3 Put the dough on a floured
table. Push your hands into the
dough, gather it into a ball and turn
it again and again for 5 minutes.

4 Shape the dough into rolls (see
next page). Put them on to the
greased baking tray. Then put
them in a warm place*.

5 When the rolls have doubled
in size, then you can decorate
them however you want (see the
next page).

6 Bake them for 15 to 20 minutes.
They are done if they sound
hollow when tapped underneath.
Put them on the wire rack to cool.

210 ml (⅜ pint) warm water

*350 g (12 oz)
strong white flour*

Ask an adult for a suitable, warm place. 29

TWIST AND ROLL

You can make bread rolls in all sorts of different shapes. You can vary them even more by using different seeds to make crunchy toppings.

To make the rolls, break the bread dough into eight pieces, all about the same size, then follow the instructions on the right. Remember that the baked rolls will be twice as big as the dough, because they will grow when rising.

TORTOISE ROLL

Stick tiny balls of dough around a roll to look like four legs, a head and a tail. Mark the top of the roll to look like a shell.

PRICKLY HEDGEHOG

Make a pointed snout shape at one end of a roll. Snip the rest of the roll, the hedgehog's body, with scissors to make prickles.

Decorating the rolls

When the rolls have risen and are ready to bake, you can decorate them with any of the things shown below. To give the rolls a golden brown glaze, you will also need a beaten egg and a pastry brush.

Flower roll sprinkled with caraway seeds

You will need

Sesame seeds

Caraway seeds

1 beaten egg

Poppy seeds

Currants

Brush the rolls lightly with the beaten egg. Sprinkle seeds over them and press them gently into place. The rolls are now ready to go into the oven (see the previous page).

Prickly hedgehog with currant eyes and nose

Cottage roll sprinkled with poppy seeds

30

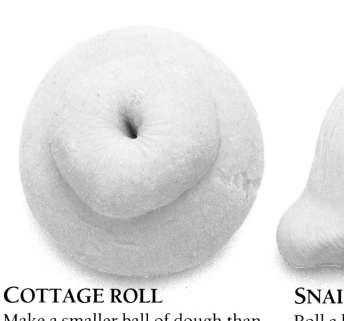

COTTAGE ROLL

Make a smaller ball of dough than the others. Brush the base of it with water. Stick it to a larger roll and make a dent in the top.

SNAIL ROLL

Roll a ball of dough into a sausage shape. Brush one side of it with water and wind it into a coil, leaving one end as the head.

FLOWER ROLL

Flatten a ball of dough slightly. Snip all round the edge of the dough with kitchen scissors to make petal shapes.

The finished rolls on a cooling rack

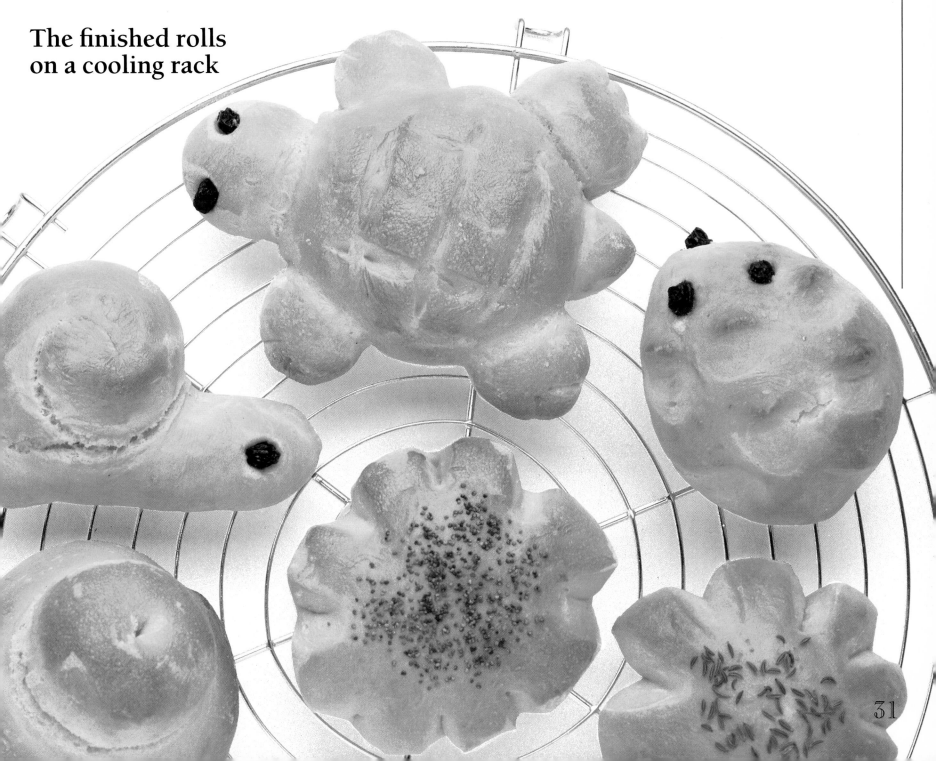

BREAD BEARS

You can make these bears using the recipe on page 28, but you need to double the ingredients given. You can also use a mixture of white and wholemeal flour. When you have made the dough, break it into three different-sized balls. Apart from the dough, you will need decorating ingredients, a large, greased baking tray and kitchen scissors or a knife.

You will need for decoration

1 beaten egg

Sesame seeds   *Poppy seeds*

Currants

Grated cheese

Making the bears

1 Break a ball of dough in two. Roll half of it into a big ball for the bear's body. Put it on the baking tray and flatten it a little.

2 Break the remaining dough in two. Roll half of it into a small ball. Roll the other half into a sausage shape 15 cm (6 in) long.

3 Brush one side of the small ball with egg. Stick it to the bear's body, tucking it slightly underneath to make the head.

4 Break off a piece of the roll. Brush one side of it with egg and stick it to the bear's face. Pinch it to make it look like a snout.

5 Cut two small pieces for the ears and four bigger ones for the legs. Pinch them into position under the bear's body and head.

6 Using the kitchen scissors or a knife, snip or slash the ends of the bear's legs to make them look like paws with claws.

Letting the bears rise

7 Make all the bears this way. Cover them loosely with a tea-towel and leave them in a warm place to rise for about an hour, until they have doubled in size. Then brush them lightly with beaten egg to glaze them, and use currants to make their eyes. Now you can add other decorations if you like.

Cooking the bears

8 Bake the bears in the oven (see page 29) for 20–25 minutes, depending on their size, until they are golden brown. Then put them on to a wire rack to cool.

MUMMY BEAR

Currants for eyes

Mummy bear was brushed with beaten egg, and then sprinkled with sesame seeds.

DADDY BEAR

Currants for eyes

BABY BEAR

Currants for eyes

Daddy bear was brushed with beaten egg and then sprinkled with grated cheese before being baked.

Baby bear was brushed with beaten egg and then decorated with poppy seeds.

33

PERFECT PASTRY

Here and on the next five pages you can find out how to make tiny fruit tarts and savoury quiches. These two pages show you how to make the pastry cases. These quantities will make about thirty small tarts, depending on the size of the tins you use.

You will need

25 g (1 oz) caster sugar (for sweet tarts only)

About 3 tablespoons water

100 g (4 oz) margarine or butter

A pinch of salt

COOK'S TOOLS

Mixing bowl

Knife

Fork

Rolling pin

Wooden spoon

Pastry cutter

Patty tin or little tartlet tins

Wire rack

225 g (8 oz) plain flour

Making the pastry

1 Turn the oven on to 200°C/ 400°F/Gas Mark 6. Put the flour, butter and salt in the mixing bowl. Cut up the butter.

2 Rub the flour and butter together with your fingertips until they look like breadcrumbs. For sweet tarts, add the sugar.

3 Now mix in the water, a little at a time. You should have a soft ball of dough that leaves the sides of the bowl clean.

4 Sprinkle flour on to the table and your rolling pin. Put the dough on to the table and roll it out until it is quite thin.

5 Stamp circles out of the pastry, using a pastry-cutter or cup. The circles should be a bit bigger than your tart tins.

6 Lay each circle of pastry over a tin. Gather in the edges and press the pastry into place so that it fits the tin.

For sweet tarts

7 Prick the bases of the pastry cases with a fork. Put them in the oven and bake them for 15 minutes, until golden brown.

8 Let the tins cool, then lever the pastry cases out with a knife and put them on to a wire rack. See how to fill them over the page.

For savoury tarts

9 Add the filling now (see pages 38–39). Then put the tarts in the oven to bake for about 20 minutes, until the filling sets.

Turn to the next four pages for filling ideas.

Fruit Tarts

To make these fruit tarts, cook the pastry cases first (see the previous page). Then fill them with fruit and glaze them with melted jam. It is best to use soft fruits like those shown below, because you don't have to cook them.

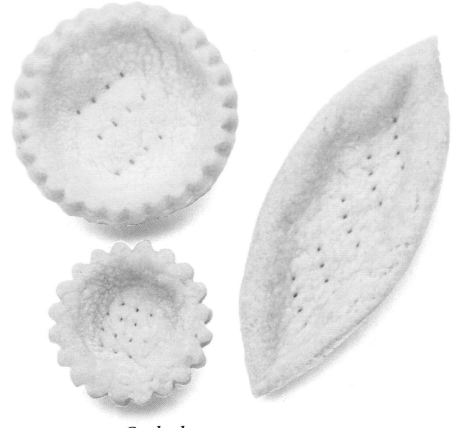

You will need

450 g (1 lb) fruit, such as:

Cooked, sweet pastry cases

Tinned or fresh pineapple

Raspberries

Blackberries

Seedless grapes

COOK'S TOOLS

Wooden spoon

Small saucepan

Sharp knife

Pastry brush

Tinned mandarin oranges

100 g (4 oz) redcurrant jelly (or sieved apricot jam)

Filling the tarts

1 Make a glaze for the tarts by melting the redcurrant jelly or sieved apricot jam in the small saucepan over a low heat.

2 Brush the insides of the pastry cases with the glaze. Wash the fresh fruit and drain the tinned fruit. Cut the grapes in half.

3 Arrange the fruit in the pastry cases, as shown below. Then brush the fruit with the glaze, which will set as it cools.

The finished tarts

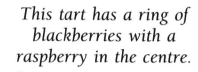

This tart has a ring of blackberries with a raspberry in the centre.

Arrange mandarin orange segments so they overlap to form a circle.

Use slices of grape, four pineapple segments and a grape for the centre.

Use pineapple, mandarin segments, raspberries and halved grapes.

The grape in the centre of this is put between two chunks of pineapple.

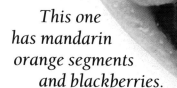

This one has mandarin orange segments and blackberries.

Mini Quiches

When making quiches or savoury tarts, put the filling in the pastry cases before you cook them. You can add whatever you want to the basic filling of eggs and milk to give the quiches any flavour you like. Try combinations of the filling ingredients shown below.

You will need

2 eggs

200 ml ($\frac{1}{3}$ pt) milk

Uncooked, unsweetened pastry cases (see pages 34 to 35)

Chopped spring onions

Plus any of these ingredients

Sliced tomatoes

Strips of sliced ham

Finely sliced leeks

Sliced mushrooms

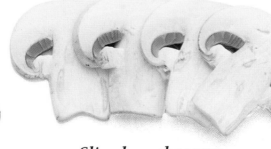

Tinned tuna fish

Grated cheese

Cook's Tools

- Knife
- Fork
- Cheese-grater
- Chopping board
- Measuring jug

What you do

1 Slice the tomatoes and mushrooms. Chop the ham and spring onion. Drain the tuna and sweetcorn. Grate the cheese.

2 Break the eggs into the measuring jug. Beat them well with the fork. Pour in the milk and whisk the mixture together.

3 Arrange the fillings in the pastry cases, pour on the egg mixture. Put them in the oven for 20 minutes (see page 35).

The finished quiches

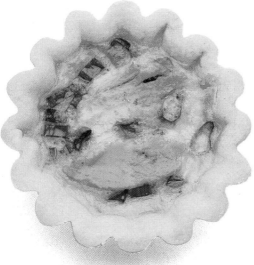

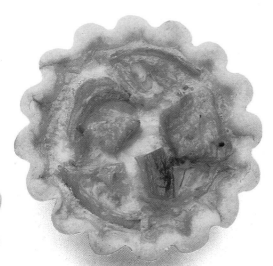

This quiche is filled with a mixture of tuna fish and spring onion.

Tinned tuna fish and sliced tomatoes are used in this quiche.

Place sliced leeks in this quiche. Then put strips of ham on top.

This quiche has grated cheese topped with sliced tomatoes.

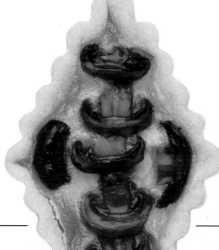

In this quiche sliced mushrooms are arranged to overlap slightly.

Chocolate Dips

You can make delicious homemade sweets by dipping your favourite fruits and nuts into melted chocolate. Make sweets out of the things shown below and put them in pretty sweet papers to give away as presents. You can also use them to decorate a special cake, or best of all – just enjoy eating them!

Cook's Tools

- **Small bowl**
- **Small saucepan**
- **Wooden spoon**
- **Cocktail sticks**
- **Waxed paper**
- **Paper sweet cases**

You will need

150 g (6 oz) plain chocolate

Cherries

Mandarin segments

Brazil nuts

Blanched almonds

Walnuts

Melting the chocolate

1 Break the chocolate up into a bowl. Heat some water in the saucepan over a low heat until it just begins to bubble.

2 Stand the bowl over the saucepan over a low heat. Stir the chocolate with a wooden spoon until it completely melts.

3 Turn off the heat. Very carefully move the saucepan and the bowl from the stove to a mat or teatowel.

Strawberries

Dipping the fruit and nuts

4 One at a time, put a piece of fruit on a cocktail stick and dip half of it into the chocolate. Then put it on to waxed paper to dry.

5 Using your fingers, dip the nuts halfway into the melted chocolate, one at a time. Let them dry on the waxed paper.

Seedless grapes

Arranging your sweets

You can put the finished sweets in paper sweet cases. If they are for a special occasion, arrange them in circular patterns on a large plate.

41

SURPRISE CAKE

For birthdays, parties and other celebrations it is nice to make a special cake. Or you can make a cake, just because you want to give someone a surprise. Here is a recipe for a delicious and light sponge cake that you can decorate however you like. You can find out how to make the cake below, and then turn to the next four pages to see how to ice and decorate it in different ways.

You will need

150 g (6 oz) softened butter

150 g (6 oz) plain flour

Making the cake

1 Set the oven at 180°C/350°F/ Gas Mark 4. Rub some butter around the insides of the two sandwich tins thoroughly.

2 Put the softened butter and sugar in the mixing bowl. Beat them with the wooden spoon until the mixture is pale and creamy.

3 Beat the eggs in a small bowl. Add them to the butter and sugar mixture a little at a time stirring it in well until it is smooth.

3 eggs

150 g (6 oz) caster sugar

COOK'S TOOLS

Mixing bowl

Fork

Wooden spoon

2 20-cm (8-inch)
Sandwich cake tins

Small bowl

Wire rack

1½ teaspoons baking powder

4 Sift the flour and baking powder into the mixture and mix well. The cake mixture should be soft and light.

5 Pour half of the cake mixture into each sandwich tin and smooth it level. Place the tins in the oven for 20 to 25 minutes.

6 The cakes are done when well-risen and brown. They should feel springy in the middle. Turn them out on to a wire rack to cool.

Now turn the page.

PICTURE CAKE

This cake is filled and topped with chocolate butter icing and decorated. Copy the sweet hen, or make up a new picture.

*Turn the page for another decorated cake.

You will need

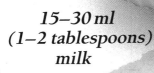

15–30 ml
(1–2 tablespoons)
milk

COOK'S TOOLS

Sieve

Mixing bowl

Knife

Wooden spoon

15 ml (1 tablespoon) cocoa powder

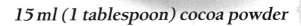

75 g (3 oz) softened butter

150 g (6 oz) icing sugar

Icing the cake

1 Put the butter in the bowl and cut it into small pieces. Beat it hard with the wooden spoon until it is soft and creamy.

2 Sift the icing sugar and cocoa powder into the bowl, a little at a time, mixing them in with the butter. Then stir in the milk.

3 When the cakes are cool, spread half the icing on one of them. Put the other cake on top and spread the rest of the icing over it.

Arranging the sweet hen

4 Now decorate the cake. Press the sweets firmly into the icing. Start with the border, do the nest and arrange the hen last of all.

Hundreds and thousands

Blanched almonds

Coloured chocolate sweets

Chocolate drops

The finished cake

Almond beak

Almond tail

Chocolate drops

Orange chocolate sweet

Sweet border

Hundreds and thousands

45

Frosted Flower Cake

You will need

This cake is filled with jam and topped with icing and crystallized grapes and flowers. We have used rose petals, but you can use any small flowers if they are safe to eat, (ask your parents first). The flowers and fruit take 2 to 3 hours to dry, so allow time.

1 egg

White icing, using 175 g (7 oz) icing sugar and 3 tablespoons of hot water

What to do

1 Crack the egg over a bowl. Slip the yolk from one half of the shell to the other, so that the white slips into the bowl.

2 Whisk the egg white until it is frothy. On a wire rack placed over a plate, paint the rose petals and grapes with egg white.

3 Sprinkle sugar over the rose petals. Dip the grapes into the sugar to coat them. Then leave the rose petals and grapes to drain.

COOK'S TOOLS

Pastry brush

Teaspoon

2 Bowls

Knife

Whisk

Wire rack

4 Spread each cake with jam and sandwich them together. Make the icing and spread it over the top of the cake, with a wet knife.

5 Arrange the rose petals and grapes on the cake before the icing sets. They will stick to the cake as the icing dries.

46

The recipe for plain white icing is on page 14.

Bowl of caster sugar

Rose petals or small flowers

Grapes

Apricot jam

The finished cake

Crystallized grapes

Crystallized petals

Crystallized petals

CHOCOLATE TRUFFLES

These truffles are delicious and very gooey. The ingredients shown make about eight truffles, so double or treble the quantities to make more.

You will need

25 g (1 oz) cocoa powder

50 g (2 oz) icing sugar

50 g (2 oz) soft cheese

What to do

1 Put the cheese, chopped nuts, icing sugar and cocoa powder in the mixing bowl and stir them until everything is well mixed.

50 g (2 oz) chopped nuts

2 Now roll the mixture into marble-sized balls in the palms of your hands. You can make them bigger if you like.

Rolling the truffles

3 Sprinkle the table with vermicelli and carefully roll the truffles in it. Then put each one in a sweet case.

Chocolate vermicelli

The finished truffles